MW01062009

How to Observe Your Group

3rd Edition

by Hedley G. Dimock

CAPTUS PRESS

How to Observe Your Group, 3rd Edition

Canadian Cataloguing in Publication Data

Dimock, Hedley G., 1928–
   How to observe your group

3rd ed.
Includes bibliographical references.
ISBN 1–895712–38–6

1. Small groups. 2. Sociometry. 3. Social groups.
I. Title.

HM133.D55 1993   302.3'4   C93–094100–4

ISBN 1–895712–38–6

First Edition, 1970; Second Edition, 1985
First Captus Press Edition, 1992
Third Edition, 1993

Copyright © 1993 by Hedley G. Dimock
           and Captus Press Inc.

All rights reserved. No part of this publication may be reproduced, stored in a retrieval system, or transmitted, in any form or by any means, electronic, mechanical, photocopying, recording, or otherwise, without prior permission of the author and Captus Press Inc.

Captus Press Inc.
York University Campus
4700 Keele Street
North York, Ontario
M3J 1P3 Canada
Phone: (416) 736–5537
FAX: (416) 736–5793

0 9 8
Printed in Canada

Table of Contents

Preface

As I write this third edition and fifth revision of *How to Observe Your Group*, I am reminded that I wrote the first edition in 1962 after I had been teaching elementary and high school courses, directing residential programs, teaching nurses, YMCA staff and social agency workers for ten years. The original book was written for "workers in community serving organizations." Over the years the readership has changed to include a broader spectrum of community serving organizations (health services, education, recreation, and social and community programs), and each revision has reflected that change. As this is the all time best seller of my ten books I have tried to keep pace with this broadening readership yet not lose the focus of "people working with people." Lately, the book has been used in management and organizational behavior courses where students form groups to do business simulations and case studies. Students' learning has as much to do with their work group's effectiveness as does the course content and instructors have students read *How to Observe Your Group* to introduce them to small group dynamics.

My other reflection on the thirty years since the first edition is the shifting priority on group observation skills. In the early years most human service workers were expected, if not required, to have training or take courses in working with groups. This trend culminated during the late 1960s when so many people in the human services, and also in business, industry and government were in small group experiential training (T-groups, encounter groups and sensitivity training). As the fad died out during the 1970s so did a lot of the trendy interest in group observation. The 1980s brought a renewed interest in groups as "Japanese style management" (Americans had invented it but not used it) and quality work circles swept North America. Everyone quickly found a renewed interest in group observation; for if the small group dynamics were not understood and managed, the new approach was just a waste of time.

At this time what was learned from previous years have been consolidated into a recognition that the success of almost everything having to do with people has to do with the understanding and effectiveness of the groups to which they belong. And while local governments have long recognized this principle, provincial and federal government agencies have been brought back to this reality by the disillusionment of the 1990s and the rejection of many of their plans. The recession in the early part of the decade has also intensified the interest of the human services and business in increasing productivity through more observant and effectively led work groups.

Hedley G. Dimock
Puslinch, Ontario
March, 1993

<table>
<tr><td>

PART ONE

</td><td>

Some Ways of Looking at Group Development

</td></tr>
</table>

A framework or theory of how groups grow and develop is needed to determine areas for observation—what we are going to look for in a group depends on what we think is important. A framework around which to view a group's development is also necessary to understand groups, make predictions about groups, communicate with others about what's happening in the group, and help groups become more effective. Six group development theories are presented here to illustrate the most widely accepted viewpoints and to provide a solid framework of alternative concepts from which readers can select the ones that make the most sense to them. All of these viewpoints have been used extensively by the author in his teaching, training and consulting to help designated leaders and members understand what typically happens in their groups. I shall use the term *designated leader* to mean the person who is, in the eyes of the group members, supposed to be the head of the group—usually an assigned or formal leader. This designated leader may be: a supervisor, a chairperson, a unit head, a director, a president or an advisor. Thus, in most groups, the designated leader will be a more senior, or higher-ranking staff person, but in some groups will be a president or chairperson who has been elected or appointed by the group.

Another book in this series, *Factors in Working with Groups*,[1] emphasized that all behaviour has some purpose or goal—people don't just 'do things.' If all the behaviour of members in your group has some purpose, it helps to try to figure out what the pay off is to understand the behaviour. And the best place to start looking is with the REAPS model of emotional needs. Of the five needs

RECOGNITION
EXPERIENCE
APPROVAL
POWER
SECURITY

those most frequently in play in the group's dynamics are *power* (about 75% of time) and recognition (about 15% of the time). When you are looking at an aggressive dominator or a dogmatic, reactionary blocker,

---

1. Hedley G. Dimock, *Factors in Working with Groups*, 2nd ed. (North York: Captus Press, 1992).

1

think *power*. And when you are looking at the posturing egalitarian or the flighty supporter of all positions, think *recognition*.

The attempts of participants to meet their needs in the group most often shows up in the *process* dimension. At any time in the group there is the *content*—what it is that the members are discussing or the activity they are working on. And the *process*—how the group is working and how the members are relating to one another. I call these the "words and the music." The words are the content and the music is the process and it is the music or process that the sharp eyed observer is looking at. The extended bickering over when to break for coffee or the minutes of the last meeting are a huge waste of time and make no sense when looked at from a *content* perspective, but the *music* clarifies they are considered as conflicts over power at the interpersonal, process level. Alfred Hitchcock, the director of many spellbinding movies, clarified this idea: "When I say that I'm not interested in content, it's the same as a painter worried about whether the apple he's painting is sweet or sour. Who cares?"

Yes, who cares? It's in the group's process where the important dynamics in the development of the group take place. The observation skills described here will increase your influence in the group and help you gain more recognition and status by helping you understand the group's dynamics. And you'll be more effective in making interventions to help move the group forward.

Viewpoint I—Developmental Areas

The two major contributions of a framework of group development are to identify the areas that are worth observing, and to help explain the relationship among various happenings in the group. The areas of group development identified in this viewpoint are the ones I have used most extensively in my work. They have been regularly updated and were revised again for this edition to reflect their extensive use by nurses, adult educators, managers, group workers and volunteer youth leaders.

The five areas presented in this viewpoint are:

- Climate
- Involvement
- Interaction
- Cohesion
- Productivity

These five areas provide a crisp yet comprehensive overview and while they represent a systems theory of groups, they can be used with the other five developmental models presented here. It has been found that by observing, understanding, and giving attention to these five areas, groups can improve their procedures, accomplish more of their goals, and provide more satisfaction for participants of their own

2

needs and interests. (See the Group Observation Guide on p. 36 that accompanies this viewpoint.)

Group Climate

Group climate includes both the physical climate or set up and the emotional climate which can be equally important to the well-being and growth of the group. The physical surroundings should encourage the work of the group—its task accomplishment and morale of the members. Seating arrangements, lighting, ventilation, proximity of members and pleasantness of the surroundings can all affect the group. A gym floor is a poor location for a small group planning session, a theatre style classroom is a poor place for a teachers meeting, and rows of benches in a lunch room do not lend themselves to a board meeting. Moving outdoors to a shady area of grass makes for pleasant surroundings but reduces attention span and interaction possibilities. Tables and chairs increase the orderly decision making activities of a group, yet an open circle of chairs may result in more personal communication and expression of feeling. Non-verbal communication is quite important in some groups and if all the members can't see one another, such a group would be handicapped much the same as a group where members couldn't all hear one another.

Perhaps even more important is the emotional climate of the group which determines the security and acceptance of members. A friendly, informal, accepting climate can encourage trust among members and, by decreasing anxiety, help members to take risks and use their resources. Expectations for the group by the organization (rules and regulations), and the style of the designated leader can also influence group climate.

Group Involvement

Involvement refers to the extent that members are occupied or absorbed with the group. Involvement is usually determined by attraction to the other members in the group and to the activities or product of the group. Involvement may also be encouraged through the overall status and power the group has in the community. Having some stake in the outcome of the group's work also increases involvement.

The key questions in assessing involvement are: why are the members here; what attracts them to the group; what level of commitment do they have to the group; and what personal needs are they meeting by belonging? Levels of involvement show up in lateness, absenteeism and turnover, and inattention and noncommitment to group tasks. Thus the levels of participation and involvement are closely related. Groups with high involvement are most likely to develop a sense of solidarity and cohesion, and become strong, healthy groups.

Involvement can be encouraged by increasing the attractiveness of the group's activities, the satisfactions members receive from interacting with the other members, and the prestige gained through the group's accomplishments. Opportunities for members to participate in setting their own work goals and procedures are usually very successful in increasing involvement. The use of inter-group competition, awards and prizes often increases involvement in the short term; yet if they don't relate to the real needs and interests of the members, they will quickly wear out.

Group Interaction

Interaction is a key dimension in group development, for the more members interact with one another, the more likely the group will develop and accomplish its tasks. Groups with high rates of interaction tend to be healthier and more productive than groups where there is low interaction or just interaction among sub-groups. Generally, the more people interact with each other, the more likely they are to be attracted to each other and develop solid relationships. Interaction can be encouraged by arranging the physical set up so people can see and talk easily to each other, and selecting activities that facilitate members interacting and working together. Group decision-making activities, small group team projects and coffee breaks promote more interaction than library work or listening to a speech.

Emotional climate is closely related to interaction. Members who feel secure and accepted in a group setting are encouraged to interact with others and to express some of their real feelings, problems and concerns. Relationship problems, sub-group conflict and the status hierarchy may get in the way of free interaction. An analysis of the roles of group members described as Viewpoint II gives a great deal of information about the interaction of a group.

Group Cohesion

Cohesion, the fourth major dimension of group growth, is often called solidarity or unity. It relates to the strengths of the relationships among the members, and can be assessed by determining how well members know and understand each other, and by the degree of feeling they have for the group as their own. In many ways, cohesion is a product of climate, involvement and interaction. There are groups where cohesion is high, but interaction may not be well distributed or the emotional climate may create insecurity.

Groups with a high degree of solidarity or cohesion are most able to encourage deviant members to accept or compromise with group standards through the group pressure they can exert. Behaviour and attitudes are most likely to be influenced in rather highly cohesive groups that are attractive to the individual members.

A growing group generally becomes more cohesive, although occasionally a group can become too cohesive for its own good, as when members refuse to admit any newcomers. At this stage of standing pat and keeping the same membership, the group may not continue to grow and mature.

A cohesive group pulls together towards common objectives. It is this solidarity that helps the group to maintain itself as a group and

4

provides the pressure to encourage members to conform to group standards and work toward common goals. It provides the glue that holds the group together and enables it to achieve its goals.

Group Productivity

The productivity and accomplishments of a group provide much of the motivation for membership and are usually the focus for group interaction. All groups are seen by their members as having goals or tasks to accomplish, and the movement toward these goals influences the satisfaction of the members and the pride in the group as a whole. It is important to study the origin of a group's goals; the integration of individual goals into group goals; the plans or procedures, if any, designed to facilitate the accomplishment of these goals; and the ability of the group to follow the plans and achieve the goals. This involves areas of goal setting, goal clarification, gaining member commitment, decision making and implementation.

Styles of leadership within the group and the distribution of member roles play an important part in productivity. As *Factors in Working with Groups* suggests, the appropriateness of leadership style in relation to the situational factors of the group is a major influence on group morale and productivity. Therefore, all identified roles in the group—chairperson, advisor, coach, recorder, supervisor or instructor—should be examined closely to note their impact on the group and its effectiveness.

This approach to group development suggests that there are five major group dimensions which are closely related to one another, and together account for most of the dynamics in any group. As these areas are assessed, analyzed and understood, and facilitative plans are worked out in a systematic fashion, a group can be helped to grow, increasing the satisfaction of members and the task accomplishments of the group. An observation guide is presented on page 36 of this book that lays out the major points to be assessed under these five headings.

Viewpoint II—Member Roles

Leadership may be defined in functional terms as acts which help the group to accomplish its goals or maintain itself as a group. All interactions within a group may be classified as helping the group to accomplish its task, helping the group to maintain itself as a group, or not serving any group function.

The viewpoint of group development from the roles of its members implies that a group needs both task and group building oriented participation of members if it is to grow and become fully productive (see Figure 1). All participation can be recorded and classified as one or another of the fourteen functions or roles. The observation sheet shown on pages 44–45, has fourteen areas in which to classify the verbal interactions of the members. The divisions are as follows:

5

FIGURE 1   *Productivity Using Task Roles vs. Group Roles*

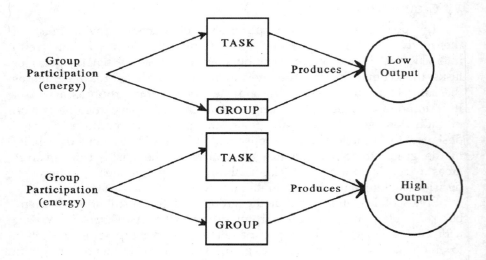

Giving major attention to task roles produces lower output (productivity) than giving attention to both task and group roles.

Task Roles
1. Defines problems
2. Seeks information
3. Gives information
4. Seeks opinions
5. Gives opinions
6. Tests feasibility

Group Building and Maintenance Roles
7. Coordinating
8. Mediating-harmonizing
9. Orienting-facilitating
10. Supporting-encouraging
11. Following

Individual Roles (Non-functional)
12. Blocking
13. Out of Field
14. Digressing

Not only does a group need both task and group building functions, but it needs appropriate functions at the right time. When a

FIGURE 2 *Role Development Over Time*

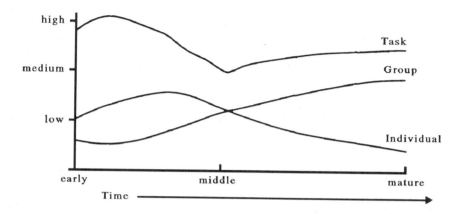

Mature groups show a reasonable balance of task and group roles. Individual roles increase in the early stages of development and drop off during the mature stage.

---

football team isn't functioning well, an analysis is made of the different player positions. The centre may be snapping the ball a bit late or the guards may not be blocking their men. All of the roles need to function well if the team is to operate smoothly and win games. In a football squad a man is assigned to each position and he knows his job. But a group may have many roles or functions that are not played and the members may not be aware of these omissions. A review of the roles taken in the group compared to the roles that a group requires (such as the eleven task and group building roles) points up the gaps. Filling the gap requires recognition of the importance of these roles or group positions and the ability of the members to take these roles when needed. The ability to take a wide variety of roles as they are needed in different situations is called role flexibility and is likely to be the most valuable attribute of a fully functioning group member.

The extent to which the eleven essential functions are taken becomes evident through group observation. The performance of these functions may be poorly spread around the group with only two or three people attempting to fill all the positions. This keeps other members from assuming responsibility and is unlikely to utilize the skills of all the members. Members may not have the opportunity to practice new roles and grow accordingly, if two or three people dominate. And if there is domination by a few, the resources of new members are not utilized.

Role flexibility, inadequate role distribution and missing group functions, once identified through observation and analysis, can be improved by discussion and agreement of group needs, and the practice of the needed roles in the group. Individual training through reality practice in out-of-group situations is also helpful.

Groups, during their initial stages of development, tend to be primarily task oriented. Almost all the participation is at a task level, such as giving opinions and giving information. The development of the group, as well as its productivity, is limited unless it can move into the group building area.

In fact, the development of a group can be charted by comparing the percentage of task roles to group building and non-functional roles. The early stages are characterized by a high proportion of task roles with individual roles growing in number. As growth progresses, group roles rise and individual roles drop off.

In summary, them, a group has to acquire a balance of task and group functions if it is to utilize all its potential as a group. Typically, groups are task oriented and need help in learning group building roles. Certain functions are required at specific times and these can often be determined through observation and analysis. It is also helpful if the roles are widely distributed among members and all assume responsibility for the functions the group requires.

The member function viewpoint of group development is of special interest to educational and therapeutic programs because of the close relation between the flexibility of an individual's functions in groups and other social situations. The healthy, well-functioning person has been described as one who is able to be flexible in social roles and behaviour. An important part of personality development is learning to take a wide variety of social roles skillfully and realistically, developing a large repertoire of them, and becoming adroit in shifting from one role to another as the situation changes.

To be sure, the eleven task and group building roles are but a few of the important social roles in life. Yet, the learning by an individual of the skills of shifting from one role to another and the ability to assess a situation to know what roles are useful is an important contribution to personal growth. Role flexibility coupled with the effective use of task and group building roles is an indicator of a flexible, adaptive person who has little susceptibility to behavioural disorders.

Viewpoint III—Interpersonal Relations

The following framework for observing, understanding and talking to others about groups is a continuation of the one started in *Factors in Working with Groups*, describing the basic needs and development of individuals. It is based on the three interpersonal needs proposed by Schutz (1958, 1966, 1989) and has been put into a developmental framework based on my experiences and those of other writers about group development. The framework assumes that groups, like individ-

FIGURE 3 *Progression Towards Mature Development*

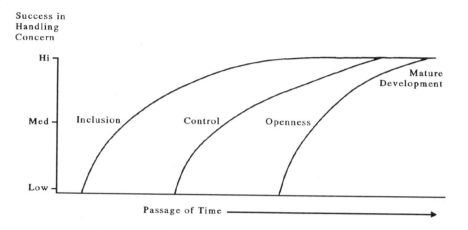

Success in
Handling
Concern

Each dimension moves forward one at a time, and each requires the previous one to be resolved before it can develop adequately.

uals, have three basic developmental needs: namely inclusion; control, and intimacy or openness. The development of a group is handicapped or arrested if each dimension is not resolved in its order of emergence. Thus a group that has not worked out the inclusion needs of its member in a reasonably satisfactory way is not likely to progress very far into the areas of control and openness. Figure 3 suggests how this works.

Figure 3 is not meant to imply that a group works on only one factor in growth at a time or always in order. Rather, it suggests a usual order of development, but once a group is underway, it moves from dimension to dimension as problems come up. In working on and managing these problems, the development of that factor is moved that much further ahead. Over a period of time, the same three issues of inclusion, control and intimacy continue to surface but at higher or more sophisticated levels. For example, in the early life of a group it may be sufficient for members to ascertain the degree of membership they hold on the group. Later, they may want to experiment with reaching out to bring in a fringe member of the group who has been a cautious participant, or add new members to the group. And later, they may want to test the quality of their acceptance in the group as they take on more authentic roles that are perhaps deviant from the usual traditional roles they first took in order to gain inclusion. These activities aimed at achieving a higher level of satisfaction of the three

FIGURE 4   *Group Growth Over Time*

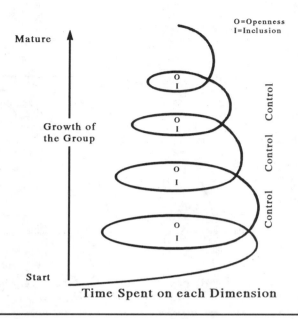

O=Openness
I=Inclusion

Mature

Growth of
the Group

Start

Time Spent on each Dimension

basic needs I refer to as The Heliotrix Phenomenon. A heliotrix is an inverted corkscrew and Figure 4 attempts to show inclusion, control and openness being dealt with at higher levels of resolution as the group matures. It also shows that as the group started work, the inclusion of participants took a fair bit of time—perhaps several meetings. But as the group went on to resolve the concerns for control and openness and later came back to improving inclusion, it took less time. In the mature phase of development the group might work on all three concerns very quickly—perhaps working on all three in one meeting.

As the group moves toward its termination, the heliotrix phenomenon works in reverse. The group leaves its openness phase, moves back to early issues of control, and concludes with a focus of inclusion namely disengagement and separation.

Most groups start off dealing with these three factors in order. My studies of project groups found that members characterized their early, middle and late phases with descriptions consistent with inclusion, control and intimacy. While a middle stage of development may include issues of inclusion and intimacy or openness, most groups describe the predominating theme as one of control.

Schutz (1966, 1989) has done some research which suggests that groups formed of members who are compatible on these three dimensions will be more effective than other groups. Thus if a group has some members who want to be in control and others willing to accept

10

that control, it will function better than a group with "all chiefs and no indians." The idea is worth thinking about. While I have not composed groups on that criteria, I have found it useful to look around groups I'm working with and ask myself (and sometimes the group) how the "chiefs" and "indians" balance out.

While it is always difficult and risky to generalize about the growth of a group without knowing its size, physical surroundings, members or goals, the following description creates a framework within which your group can be looked at and compared to other groups. The forms of expression of typical group concerns and the relationships among them may stimulate your thinking about linkages that will make sense in understanding your group. And keep in mind that during all three phases there are the 'words and the music'—what the group is talking about or apparently working on and what interpersonal concern the group may really be dealing with at that time. And, while all groups are different, I think you'll be startled to find how well these descriptions fit your group.

Inclusion Stage

During the first few meetings of a new group the members try to get to know each other to see whom they will like and who will accept them. They usually do this by talking about the weather, current events, or perhaps sharing some recent experience (I call these cocktail issues). This is an effort to establish their *inclusion* in the group and to be recognized and accepted as a member. Part of becoming a member is to know what the group expects of you so you can figure out whether you really want to belong. And it helps for the other group members to know what you expect from the group or why you want to join. As participants balance out what they will need to do and give to gain acceptance, they establish their level of commitment to group. It is important to assess likely time and financial expectations, usual procedures (will you need to use a computer?), and attitudes and values that the group personifies.

The process of finding out about the group and what it is going to expect, looking over the other participants and making some first impressions of what they are going to be like, and presenting yourself to the group as favourably as you can is difficult and scary. Some participants find this "getting acquainted" process easiest if they jump into the activities or discussion, while others find that sitting back and watching works best for them. This creates a split between over- and under-participators and often becomes an issue in the group as the big talkers try to pressure the quiet members into talking more. While the *words* are about appropriate participation in the group, the *music* is about what participants need to do to become accepted members of this group (who's in/who's out).

Participants may also ask about the goals of the group, the background of the organization to which the group belongs, and the qualifications of the designated leader as a way of sorting out what is going to be expected of them. Some groups try to facilitate this process by having orientation sessions to review goals and procedures, and tell the participants what is expected of them. Sometimes, too, there is a formal initiation and acceptance ceremony. These structuring activities may help but members still need to work out shared expectations and figure out who in the group likes them and who they are going to like. I have also seen groups, especially those composed of professional people-workers, try to ignore these give/get inclusion concerns and move directly onto specific tasks. This theory assures us that it is not going to work out and that they will soon be back to the unresolved inclusion needs they tried to skip.

As this individually-oriented phase moves toward closure, members are usually able to name those who are solidly in the group, those who are half way in, and who are still on the fringe. Groups that feel inclusion is unresolved may set attendance requirements (miss two meetings in a row and you're out) or other artificial regulations to try and help. At this time, too, members may resist taking in any new members and treat outsiders cooly as ways of protecting the inclusion comfort they have worked so hard to establish. All in all, this phase is a time of hope and trepidation.

Control Stage

The group leaves the inclusion stage with a pretty clear picture of the acceptance level of each member. In the control phase members are trying to work out "who gets to decide what for whom." This means establishing who in the group has what amount of power—determining the power hierarchy. I call it working out the "pecking order"—the order in which chickens feed. As attention shifts to decision making and to who has influence, there is a fair amount of aggression and conflict as members jockey for position in the control hierarchy.

The relevance of the topics discussed increases during this stage and usually includes how the group will make decisions—majority vote, general agreement, or everyone has to agree. While the *words* do become more important it is clearly the *music* that is the real focus and determines successful development. Disillusionment with the group as it bickers leads to discontent—"the group is getting nowhere." Members talk a lot about leaving the group but rarely do.

During the control phase there can be a lot of bickering over very minor points as members attempt to consolidate their positions in the group. Sometimes a member will try to take over the group (which makes the group safe for that person), but the group will not allow it for very long. Another play to make the group safe is to prevent any decision-making procedures from being established and then no one will have to do anything they do not want to do. This can be a more difficult problem to handle, it may leave the group powerless—an arrested group.

Once the power and influence hierarchy is established and some agreement is reached about how group decision will be made, members relax a bit and start enjoying themselves. Any "pecking order", even if you come in last, is better than none, as ambiguity about position and continuous conflict in pushing for a position is totally unsettling.

Groups that work through these control issues at an adequate level are able to share the leadership functions among all the members and are consequently able to utilize the full resources in the group. No Single member becomes indispensable and all share in accepting responsibility. As the group increases its solidarity during this phase and sets challenging but attainable goals, it also develops standards for its members which help to facilitate the movement towards agreed upon goals. As a result, the work level or productivity of the group increases.

With satisfactory solutions to the problems in the control area, there is a great sense of accomplishment in the group. This may create a very high happiness level where the group feels it is really great and attempts to maintain this group harmony past the point of usefulness. As far as the group is concerned, there is no project too challenging, no task too difficult for it to handle. The recognition that this attitude is unrealistic and there are other things to accomplish leads to the next stage of openness and member authenticity.

Openness Stage

The major concern during this stage of group development is working out how open or authentic members are prepared to be with one another considering the purposes of the group. The group starts giving less attention to the status hierarchy and the key players, and more attention to the ideas and unique abilities of each member. There is an acceptance of individual differences and less concern about deviants conforming to group standards as this stage is successfully resolved. The creative members of the group play an increasingly important role and leadership shifts among members in terms of the group task or situation at hand.

As readiness to give and take for the good of the group increases, members volunteer to work with one another in task groups on the basis of who would be helpful in doing the job (rather than the who likes whom of the inclusion phase). Old Taylor, generally excluded during the inclusion stage because of his reactionary views is now included for his "historic perspective". Members now see the development of the group in perspective and laugh at the antics of the inclusion and control stages.

Members of the group feel secure with one another and as the trust level develops, there is more sharing of real feelings. This authentic communication and intimacy increases the attraction of the group for members. As personal feelings and opinions are communicated in a direct and open fashion, the data available for problem solving rapidly increases. Efficiency rises as no time is wasted trying to figure out what participants are really saying, or worrying about what strategy is being used on the group. Now each member can be known and treated as an individual, and the unique abilities of each member can be used for the betterment of the group. As the group is no longer hung up on power and control, it may give up 'majority rule' and move to group concensus, where all members are committed to action and taking responsibility for implementation. Resolving conflict is no longer the concern it was during the control stage. With the new level of trust and openness, it can be used creatively for the good of the group.

Termination

As the group moves toward closure there is an increase of anxiety and unsureness. During their final few work periods many groups regress to immature behaviour that was typical of the early life of the group—power struggles, bickering and questioning the real commitment of some members. There may be an attempt to downplay the importance of the group and friendships with other members as a way of easing the separation.

In a final attempt to postpone the termination of a group, a reunion or get-together at a later time will be suggested. Most groups realize that this is an artificial effort and, after discussing it, turn it down or just leave it up in the air (the realistic members will say they are too busy and no time when everyone can come will be found). Reunions don't usually happen and, when they do, are an anticlimax— a letdown to the pride and sense of accomplishment of the mature phase of development.

Summary

Groups that have resolved the usual concerns of members in the areas of inclusion, control and openness are solid, cohesive groups with members who know where they stand in relationship to one another and to the group's tasks. Leadership is typically shared in these mature groups and the designated leader is able to assign and delegate responsibilities with member sanction. While there are clear standards and expectations, the group, because of its solidarity, can tolerate some conflict and the deviant behaviour of its diverse members. A well developed group is a learning, growing experience for its members, contributing to their self actualization, physical, and mental health.

It is probable that a few groups will not be able to resolve these basic developmental concerns and will either abort or have an arrested development. Sometimes the challenges of getting it all together is just too great and the members are not able to mobilize enough to meet the challenge. The group may be too large, have a lopsided sample of prima donnas for members, or a task assignment too tough to handle. The most frequent cause of arrested development is an unresolved control issue. Often it takes the form of one or two rebellious members with low commitment who posture as egalitarian humanists and block all decision-making to "protect individual rights".

Human Service professionals are candidates for arrested development if they are unwilling to go through the trials and tribulations of

FIGURE 5 *Summary of Viewpoint III—Interpersonal Relations*

	Inclusion	Control	Openness
Concern in Play	• Who is in/out?	• Who gets to decide what for whom?	• How do members feel about each other?
Typical Activities	• Minor issue discussions • Creating a good impression	• Jockeying for position • Testing leader	• Interpersonal feedback • Focus on goal achievement
Individual Member Concerns	• What's expected of me? • How much do I want to be a member?	• How much control do I have over myself and others?	• How safe is it to be myself in this group?
Group Growth Concerns	• What Is the commitment of each member?	• Settling the "pecking order" and decision-making procedures	• Building authentic behaviour and its acceptance
Dominant Member Feelings	• Insecurity • Excitement • Enthusiasm	• Dissatisfaction • Disillusionment • Competition	• Trust • Acceptance • Goal-orientation
Productivity	• Generally Lo but Hi spots on minor procedural issues	• Medium depending on issues used to "jockey for position"	• Hi if inclusion, control and openness resolved; Lo if group aborts

group building and imagine that they can establish trust and openness by proclamation, as that is part of their training. Experienced graduate students often have a tough time becoming a group for many of the same reasons. And during the early 1990s, the continuous external pressure of the economic recession created havoc in many previously well functioning work groups. As their organizations started laying off staff, these groups regressed to immature levels of bickering, hostility and distrust as productivity plummeted.

Hopefully, you have been rather surprised by how much like your group many of these descriptions sounded. Groups are usually rather predictable because of normative processes and self-sustaining goals. An awareness of usual developmental needs and dynamics helps members and designated leaders figure out what is happening in their group and intervene in ways that will encourage further growth and development.

Viewpoint IV—Work and Emotion

The work and emotion theory of group development started with the work of Bion at the Tavestock Institute in England (1961) and was given sequential stages for application by associates of the National Training Laboratories in Group Development in the United States (Stock and Thelen, 1958; Bennis, 1964). The theory has been used extensively in classroom groups, human relations training groups, industrial work groups, and community groups. In order to understand group phenomena, the activities of the group are analyzed in terms of the *level of work* (a little to a lot) and emotional content. The emotional content is assessed on the continuums of fight vs. flight, pairing vs. counter-pairing, dependency vs. counter-dependency, or some combination of these three dimensions.

> *Flight*—Avoidance or denial of the problem, issue or task.
> *Fight*—Hostility and assertion, a direct confrontation of the problem.
> *Pairing*—Expression of intimacy, acceptance and supportiveness.
> *Counter-pairing*—Rejecting warmth and supportiveness of others.
> *Dependency*—Reliance on a person (leader, teacher, supervisor) or thing external to membership (policies, experts, regulations).
> *Counter-dependency*—Rejection or denial of authority or outside influences.

These categories may be used to describe the group as a whole, e.g., 'the group is in a state of flight', or an individual, 'Dale appears to be very dependent on the designated leader.'

Now the work and emotional components of group life are so interrelated that one never occurs without the other. Consequently, the group is always analyzed in terms of its level of work and primary emotional theme (or themes). The emotional quality often determines the level of work and vice versa. A group where members are concerned about their status and are directing *fight* to that concern, probably produces little work. Likewise, a group with an overwhelming task might handle it with emotional *flight*. At many times a group will not be openly verbalizing an emotional theme such as flight, but the activities of the group can be understood when it is assumed that they are attempting to avoid a problem or task. For example, a group may express interest in a task and apparently be working hard at it, but the more it works, the farther it gets from accomplishing that task. This behaviour can be understood if it is viewed as *flight.*, and it can be assumed that underneath the surface the group doesn't want to accomplish the task, or is afraid to try to accomplish it for some reason. Observers must ask themselves "what is this group really trying to do?" "It is acting as if it resisted or rejected the designated leader; it is running from conflict of sub-groups" and so forth.

Phases of Group Growth

Groups vary among the emotional themes they appear to be expressing, the level of work, and its relationship to emotionality. When a group is reflective, orderly, and members are listening to one another, it is primarily in a work phase. In response to individual needs or stress it may be disorderly and hostile. At such time, the group is seen as primarily in an emotional phase.

The level of work can range from a low of being unrelated to the objectives and tasks of the group, to a high where there is active problem-solving and creative, productive work. The work level of a group usually increases as it continues to meet and emotionality recedes. While there are no exact patterns for groups, the following phases can be expected.

Early Phase

The early phase is characterized by orientations towards authority and more generally, the distribution of power in the group. The usual stereotypes that prevail during this phase are that every group needs a strong, competent leader who can move the group toward its goals. It is also believed that certain 'necessary' information should be forthcoming (job title, education, family), as each member sees other members as individuals and needs to establish their position in the hierarchy in relation to that member. This phase is characterized by concerns about authority and the usual reaction is one of dependence and flight.

If the structure of the group is seen as vague and unclear, and the designated leader seems weak and ambiguous, a search for goals and objectives—a common group task—results, yet the source of anxiety is the authority figure, not the group's goal. Weak authority figures facilitate the rise of a group member who is assertive and claims to have previous group experience. Dependence on this person works well momentarily, but is doomed to failure. During this phase most behaviour is individually oriented and the work level is low.

Middle Phase

As the early phase closes there is considerable interaction with the designated leader or authority figure in an attempt to size the person up and determine what rewards and punishments may be forthcoming from various behaviours. It is important to know how much power the designated leader will have so members will know how much power, and in which areas, is left for them to share. There is more *fight* behaviour among members as they consolidate their positions in the group (this happens in the early phase of children's groups). If the designated leader is directive and encourages dependence, the power struggle among the members is less intense as there is less power up

17

for grabs. But if the authority figure is permissive and unassertive, there will be a more intense power struggle and more counter-dependent behaviour towards the worker. It will take the form of resisting the authority of the designated leader, and playing down the value of her opinions and suggestions. There may even be some discussion about the usefulness and competence of the designated leader, and perhaps suggestions of ways the group could work well on its own.

As the leadership hierarchy becomes more firmly established, there is a lot of pairing and sub-grouping among members. Two sub-groups may compete for power at this stage and surprisingly, neither may win as power often shifts to the neutral independent group. The *pairing* builds relationships and support which makes the group more relaxed and enjoyable. The close of this phase may see a honeymoon characterized by 'sweetness and light' if the group feels it has worked through its conflicts and disagreements, and feels comfortable with the authority figure.

Mature Phase

The *pairing* and good feelings that members develop during the middle phase increases the attractiveness and cohesion of the group. Group standards evolve and there is pressure on deviants to conform to these standards. The group becomes more able to maintain itself as a group and operate smoothly within the standards it has set for itself. While the work level during the middle phase is varied, this phase sees a higher level of work and more satisfaction with the work among members.

The destructive conflict and hostility that develops during the middle phase may be managed artificially with a tacit agreement of group harmony. And like real honeymoons, this tends to cover over the expression of any differences or negative feelings. The primary challenge of this mature phase is for the group to work through the compromise and harmony veneer and free up openness and authenticity so it can use the full resources of its members. In recognizing the limitations of the group and the limitations of individual members, a group can build around them. Maturity is measured by how effectively the group manages tensions, conflicts and the deviant or creative behaviour of its members. Mature groups collect relevant data on individual and group performance and use it to revise their ways of working—trust, openness and a readiness to deal with real issues are essential if this feedback is to be used successfully.

The mature phase is one of integration, group flexibility, open expression of individual feelings, and task accomplishment. It is generally characterized as high work and *pairing*, though the group's interdependence is also evident.

In summary, the most noteworthy contribution of this theory is its clarity about the importance of working through the roles and relations with the authority figure in the group. Groups that are unable to get at and deal with this person become stunted in their growth or disintegrate. Designated leaders taking their members through this tricky and unpleasant phase can gain security in understanding that the testing behaviour and hostility has little to do with them personally. Designated leaders whose leadership styles shift from directing to coaching and facilitating in pace with the growth of the group will minimize the trauma of this experience. Effective leadership can also be seen as helping the group through these three phases that have been characterized as (1) *flight* and *dependence*, (2) *fight* and *counter-dependence* and (3) *pairing* (and interdependence).

Viewpoint V—TORI and Trust Formation

Jack Gibb's TORI theory of personal, group and organizational development is based on trust—trust in one's self, in other people, and in the organizations and structures they can create. The framework of this theory is based on four dimensions and TORI is an acronym for these key factors: Trust, Openness, Realization and Interdependence. But *trust* is the basic component on which the theory is built for it is assumed that without a continuous increase in the trust level in a group, the other three factors will not be able to develop. Gibb sees fear, a symptom of unresolved trust, as the most crippling feature in personal and group development. People grow as they increase their trust and acceptance of themselves and others. Most nonfunctional behaviour of individuals and groups can be understood as fear and the facades and defences it creates. Group experiences where members learn how to create trusting, accepting climates encourage individual development and also healthy, productive groups.

In the TORI framework there are four dimensions or modal concerns in group growth. *Acceptance* is concerned with the achievement of membership in the group based on trust. *Data flow* is concerned with opening valid, spontaneous communication in the group and translating these data into decision making and choices. *Goal formation* has to do with determining member wants and integrating them into problem solving and group action planning, with a goal of productive, creative work. *Control* is concerned with leadership, power and organizational structures that can be developed into freedom-giving, flexible forms. According to TORI theory, the most revealing aspect of a group's development is a description of the ways in which the early fears in the group are resolved by an increase in trust. The chart on TORI Group Development Process describes some of the common fears and problems of early group life and what they are replaced with as the group develops more trust in later phases.

TORI is essentially a developmental theory of group growth as there is an optimal sequence in the development of the four dimensions. Yet, the four factors are processed throughout the life of the group and continually flow together and build on each other.

19

FIGURE 6   *TORI Group Development*

Modal Concern	Individual Behaviour	Early Development	Later Development
TRUST (acceptance, membership)	• accepting self and others	• conformity	• diversity welcomed
	• trusting	• fear of adequacy	• support, encouragement
	• expressing warmth	• status seeking	• acceptance of non-conformity
	• seeing differences	• need for role definition	• trust and risk taking
OPENNESS (data flow, decision making)	• spontaneity	• strategy, caution	• clarity, directness
	• rapport	• ambiguity	• spontaneous expression
	• depth communication	• secrecy	• listening, sharing
	• disclosing	• distortion of date	• increasing feedback
REALIZATION (goal formation, productivity)	• asserting	• persuasion, advice	• involvement, creativity
	• exploring	• extrinsic motivation	• cooperation
	• clarifying own needs	• competition, rivalry	• common goals
	• achieving	• apathy, withdrawal	• enthusiasm
INTERDEPENDENCE (control, organization)	• participating	• dependency	• informality
	• cooperating	• bargaining	• flexible structures
	• giving and getting freedom	• formal rules	• little need for leaders
		• structure, channels	• roles, power irrelevant

Source: Adapted from Gibb, 1978.

FIGURE 7   *TORI Group Leaders*

Move Away From — TORI LEADERS — Move Towards

Doing what's helpful	Responding to my feelings
Modelling appropriate behaviours	Sharing all of me
Focus on motives and interpretations	Focus on experienced behaviour now
Concern for them, past and future	Concern for now (being present)
Focus on limitations of each of us and what we need to get going	Focus on the strengths and growing edges of each of us
Managing the process	Getting into the process and flow
Planning, preparation, format	Focus on doing it

Source: Adapted from Gibb, 1978.

Certainly trust and acceptance compose the catalyst for the development of the other three factors if, in fact, they aren't the essential prerequisite. Trusting is an open process and any high trust group can't help but be open to highly unpredictable and emergent outcomes. Clearly, this is the most humanistic theory I have presented and, as one of its most important contributions is its openness and flexibility, it would be inappropriate for it to predetermine the usual stages of group growth.

In keeping with this humanistic orientation, the theory also expects the designated leader to be working on the same modal concerns as part of the group. As you noticed in the chart on TORI Group Development, a mature group has integrated the leadership/managing function and does not need someone to organize, teach, manage or supervise. The basic question for a designated leader using TORI theory is 'what would I be doing if I trusted this group more? The following chart gives some suggestions.

Viewpoint VI—The Forming-Storming Model of Group Development

Probably the most popular model of group development for group participants is the Forming-Storming approach of Tuckman (1977). Certainly the quote I have heard most often from group members I have worked with is "Ah! now we are into the Storming stage of development."

21

FIGURE 8   *Group Profile*

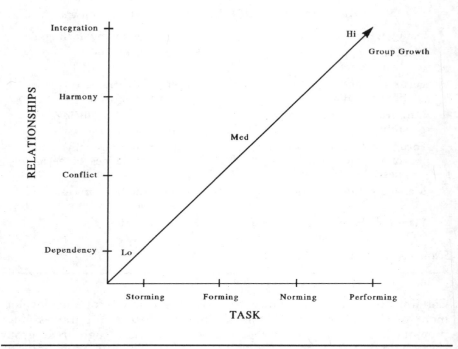

The model suggests that there are four stages of group growth:

- Forming
- Storming
- Norming
- Performing

Later Tuckman added a fifth stage:

- Adjourning

The words speak pretty much for themselves which may explain why so many people remember it.

Forming—getting started as a group and looking to the designated leader for guidance.
Storming—competition and conflict at the interpersonal level and over goals and procedures.
Norming—acceptance of other members, cooperation and building cohesion.

22

Performing—high morale based on pride of task accomplishment and richness of interpersonal relations.

Adjourning—movement toward closure: disengagement from relationships and termination of tasks.

The Forming-Storming model uses crisp, colourful words to describe its stages. The original four stages were based on a summary and analysis of fifty-five group models—about all there were at the time. Ten years later it was updated on more recent studies and the fifth stage, adjourning, added. As it does a good job of summing up so many models it serves us well as an integrative viewpoint to conclude this section (see Figure 8).

Male-Female Roles in Group Development

A careful observation and analysis over many years of typical roles taken during a group's development show some specific patterns for male and female roles during the various phases. To the extent these patterns play out in your group they add another dimension for observation and understanding. Traditional North American stereotypes are that men will be aggressive, competitive and dominant while women will be understanding, warm and affectionate. And these roles are usually seen as opposites, a person has one or the other. Sandra Bem[2] has helped us to look at the roles as two separate dimensions, a person can take on both masculine and feminine traditional roles or behaviour. Thus a supervisor may criticize a workers performance in a tough, assertive manner (stereotyped male roles) yet be sensitive and sympathetic to the disappointment and anger the criticism may create (stereotyped female roles). The blending of these roles usually though of as masculine and feminine is defined as androgyny and the person using both roles as androgynous. Thus I will describe the roles and the likely sex of the members taking them separately.

In the early phase of group development (Inclusion or Forming) the male roles are assertive—do most of the talking, and focus on the goals and tasks of the group. These people will also suggest rather structured ways to get to know each other. Some of these proposed structures will be followed by the group. In my experience, most of the people taking these roles will be men. The female roles during this stage are not very well heard in the group and as they are less

---

2. See Sandra L. Bem, "Sex-role adaptability: One consequence of psychological androgyny" (1975), 31 *Journal of Personality & Social Psychology* at 634–643; "Bem Sex-role Inventory (BSRI)" in J. Jones and J.W. Pfliffer, (eds.), *The 1977 Annual Handbook for Group Facilitators* (San Deigo, CA: University Associates, 1977); *Bem Sex-role Inventory*. (Palo Alto, CA: Consulting Psychologists Press, 1978).

frequent and low visibility have little apparent impact (but people did hear, and refer the them later).

As the pace picks up during the conflict and storming of the struggles for power and control, the males roles become more aggressive. In jockeying for position two and sometimes three people with strong male roles (usually males but sometimes a woman) will struggle hard for the top sport. They will line up people to support them and there becomes two (sometimes three) sub-groups vying for control. A lot of the members—sometimes a majority—will not join either group but will remain neutral during the sub-group's race for power. Many in this neutral group will have androgynous roles and there will be more women than men.

The two conflicting sub-groups gradually wear each other out, and the rest of the group grows tired of their bickering and is ready to move on. The catalysts for this move forward are the neutrals and the emerging leader is a person with both male and female roles.

The androgynous roles of this new leader are most helpful at this stage of development as the pecking order is established and members feel comfortable and secure enough to move on to decision-making focused on task accomplishment. The thoughful and considerate structuring this person does, along with warmth and support for others, are well received. The leadership of this person is well accepted and her status increases. This new androgynous leader is well positioned to help the others members handle the concerns of the openness or mature phase of the group's development. The flexibility of being able to perform both traditional male and female roles coupled with the respite from the aggressive, ambitious and dominating roles of the male leadership style is a winner. This person is self-reliant and independent, and can be forceful and assertive when needed (all traditional male roles), yet she or he is understanding, sympathetic and compassionate (traditional female roles). This range of roles with their suitability for the growth needs of the group makes this leader seem very authentic. This builds the trust and openness, the warmth and intimacy required to facilitate the group through the mature phase of its development.

This androgynous leader is usually a woman. In some organizations it is difficult for a woman to be seen and accepted as the leader and some groups handle this problem by appointing a male as the figurehead leader, but using the androgynous woman as the real leader or "power behind the throne." This has often been a satisfactory resolution where everyone was happy (especially if the figurehead male thinks he really is the leader). However, the elevated status and compensation awarded the figurehead, while the actual leadership resides elsewhere is becoming a sore point in many contemporary organizations. In any case, the leadership roles needed to move a group to full maturity are a combination of traditional male and female roles.

Scapegoating the Assistant Designated Leader

A phenomena somewhat related to this discussion of male-female roles in the group is the attack on the person with whom the designated leader pairs or strongly supports. My experience is confined to a male designated leader pairing or supporting a male or female who is seen as the assistant leader. But my female colleagues who are designated leaders in groups and may pair or support a male or female assistant leader tell me the same scapegoating takes place, but with less intensity—especially if she pairs with another female.

If I pair or visibly support a female member in the group—including the woman who emerges as androgynous leader as described in the preceding paragraph—she will undoubtedly be attacked with many of the feelings of disillusionment and dissatisfaction I have generated for her in pairing with me. She is seen as a substitute for me who is much safer to attack. Anger, disappointment and hostility is displaced on her and she is scapegoated for concerns related to me as the authority figure and source of power. This phenomena also takes place (although not as strongly) if I pair with or visibly support a male—perhaps because it seems less safe to attack a male substitute leader than a female; or perhaps there is less jealousy of both male and female members if it is a same-sex pairing (i.e., less perceptions of romanic overtones).

PART TWO

How to Observe Group Behaviour

"It's amazing how much you can observe by watching."
Yogi Berra

Group leadership is effective to the extent that it facilitates growth of the group and its task accomplishments. To be effective leaders and facilitators, we need to know what is going on in a group and select among our skills and resources accordingly. Direct observation is the most frequently used method to gather information about a group. Sharpening up our observation skills is a pretty sure way of making groups more effective. All of us are informal observers of the groups in which we participate, and we informally use our observations in our participation. We observe those areas that have become important to us through our many experiences, and likely pay little attention to other areas. Sharpening up our observation skills consists of broadening the variety of areas we observe, and then making our observations more systematic so that information from one meeting can be compared with similar data from other meetings. As observations are compared over a period of time, ups and downs in the group can be easily spotted and can be used for group evaluation and long range planning. If you don't know what is really going on in the group, it's difficult to lead it.

Some kind of an observation guide or set of observation categories helps to make group observations more useful by clarifying which are the important areas or dynamics to watch and focussing the observer's attention on them. There are so many things to watch in a group that no one could accurately observe half of them, and even if teams of observers watched them all, it would take hours to summarize and process the data. Which areas to select is a judgment based on previous experience but hopefully influenced by a review of suggested observation areas from the literature and the selection of some kind of framework or theory of group development. A guide also helps to make our observations more comprehensive and tends to balance out our tendency to neglect areas not important to us and to have one-sided views. A broadly focussed guide sensitizes the observer to new areas of group interaction thus checking their usefulness to the observer's frame of reference and intervention strategy.

What, then, is the most useful observation guide—the most important group dimensions to observe? It is now forty years since I made up my first observation guide and some answers are clear, though for the first twenty-five years I didn't think it made much difference what the dimensions were. Observation categories should emerge from our views of how groups grow and develop and what the most powerful dynamics are that shape that growth. There are some priority dimensions of group growth that have consistently emerged from group studies and research, and are related to most of the popular group development theories. These are summed up in the Group Observation Guide on page 36. To summarize the essential dimensions even further: focus on procedures for task accomplishment and the resulting productivity; and focus on group building and relationship activities especially those related to power and control.

Observation is the most important method for gathering information about groups because everyone related to the groups is already doing it. With our goal of refining, focussing, broadening and systematizing observations, it may be beneficial to explore the three major *kinds* of group observers. The first category is the *participant-observer* and includes everyone in the group who is using observations to help figure out what is happening in the group and to make the interventions of that persons more useful. Everyone in the group is a *participant-observer* at least unconscientiously but the term is usually reserved for those doing it purposefully.

The second category includes the *training observer* or assigned group process observer whose goal is to help the whole group understand more about what is happening in the group and motivate them to appropriate action. In the *training observer* role, the importance of the quality of the data observed decreases, as the reporting skills of the observer more usually determines success. Typically, the process observer reports periodically through a group session, or is given a chunk of time at the end of the session. The chief goal of the *training observer* is to gain acceptance for the data presentation process and stimulate further discussion and analysis of it by the group. This is facilitated by giving descriptive, non-judgmental data on the group and perhaps leaving it a bit open-ended to encourage other perspectives from the group. It is likely that these group feedback skills are harder to learn than those of basic group observation.

The third kind is the *evaluation observer* who is collecting information for performance appraisal, program evaluation and planning, or for supervising the designated leader. If the information is to be used for evaluation, it is particularly important to have standardized observation areas and recording formats to reduce observer bias and increase the comparability of many work groups, programs, or classrooms.

So You Are a New Member in a Group

How do you quickly look around and get a feeling of what's going on? You want to get accepted fast and not stick out like a country bumpkin new to the city.

27

Start by getting a first impression snapshot of the group. Look over the Group Observation Guide on page 36 and familiarize yourself with the five observation areas. Don't take it to the group with you and pull it out every few minutes—leave it at home and fill it out when you get back. This will constitute a first impression snapshot and give you an orientation to the major dynamics of the group. As Yogi Berra says, "It's amazing how much you can observe by watching," and using the Guide to focus your watching, you'll observe more than you can digest for a while.

Each group has its own personality or culture—its usual ways of doing things—that are unique and special to it as a group. The collective behaviour of the members built on the traditions of the group give it this personality. It is important to find out quickly what these "usual ways of doing things" are so you fit in if you choose to do so. These informal rules are not written down anywhere, so they take a bit of "focused watching" to figure out.

FIGURE 9   *Culture Analysis Observation Guide*

The goal is to identify the unwritten rules that determine the usual ways in which things work in this community, group or organization.

- What behaviour or activity gets rewarded? What gets demerits?

- What are the major sources of anxiety and concern?

- What are the norms for dress? Promptness? Attendance? Performance? Deadlines?

- What are the practices for handling routines, lateness, deadlines, absences, and poor performance?

- What are expectations for people to participate in and contribute to the system's well-being? ☐ Hi ☐ Med ☐ Lo

- Amount of support and encouragement given to people here?
  ☐ Hi ☐ Med ☐ Lo

- Openness/secrecy regarding: income level, competence, performance, promotions or awards, and future professional plans.

- What's talked about privately that isn't addressed publicly?

- How is unacceptable behaviour punished (sarcasm, freezing out, whispering, confrontation, rejection)?

- How are people gotten rid of here?

- How is conflict, aggressive competition, and major disagreement handled?

Source: Adapted from Dimock, 1993.

The Culture Analysis Observation Guide (Figure 9) will be helpful. Let me also stimulate your thinking of these informal rules by reporting some that I know.

- Workers arrive at their desks 20–30 minutes before starting time and read the newspaper, a book, or make personal phone calls.
- Members can raise and argue any point of view they like but must vote with the Chairperson or lose acceptance.
- Workers must wear shirt and tie, blouse and skirt on any day that there is a meeting, whatever they like (Jeans and T-shirt or Sweater) other days.
- Everyone liberates office paper, envelopes, pens, clips, etc. for home use, but nobody makes personal use of the photocopier or postage meter.
- To leave your desk and go anywhere (lunch, coffee, washroom) during the day you have to carry a file folder.
- The more clients you carried on paper (you didn't need to do anything with them) the higher your status and performance appraisal. Low status workers compensated by staying late and pushing papers around.

To be sure, some of these informal rules make no sense to the newcomer, yet at sometime there was something that started the trend and the rest of the group bought into it and made it part of the culture. Look around carefully watching the topics highlighted in Figure 9 and don't show a lot of surprise at the unusual things you may find (no one likes to have the illogical aspects of their usual ways of working laughed at).

The other area to be looking at and thinking about is what it is you need to be doing to gain membership and acceptance in this group. An understanding of what the group is going to expect of you as a member and what it is going to offer you, are the first questions in play. Then you need to check out the other members and hunch who you will pair with—who you like and think may like you. Find out what you will need to do to be a fully accepted member of this group (graduate from the initiation ceremonies and the probation status), and decide whether the gives/gets work out for you. If they do, go for it knowing you can deviate from the norms and be more of your real self after you have gained full membership and other members trust you. And, as I have described, if you can avoid aggressive competition for power while you are working out your inclusion, you will have a greater chance to be more influential later on.

In summary, try to move into the group quietly and unobstrusively by getting to know the other members individually as quickly as possible—learn everyone's name fast for you'll never coach a team if you don't know the names of the players. Take a group snapshot focusing on the procedures for task accomplishment and the group-building, relationship activities—especially those related to power and influence. Then, work on understanding the group's unique culture and unwritten rules for the usual ways of doing things.

Work hard on your own inclusion in the group and if you decide you want to be fully accepted, let others know your strong commitment to the group and its purposes. And finally, if your early impressions of the group suggest it is operating in a peculiar way that doesn't make much sense, ask yourself what the possible reason or pay-off could be for this behaviour.

- A large residential treatment program was constantly facing a crisis, moving from one crises to the next at about 2–3 month intervals. The director created these crisis to give himself directive power and to avoid dealing with everyday people concerns where he was incompetent. These crises stopped with the coming of a new director.
- An experimental, humanistic school program slowly stopped its programming and spent its time working on the personal problems and relationships of its members. The key players lacked interest and competence in the task, and the groups' problems became a substitute.

All group behaviour has some purpose, some pay off along the line. Keep looking into the group's history and ascertaining present motivations so that you can continue hunching about what the important norms and dynamics are really all about. This will lead you to working on the improvement of your observational skills.

Improving Observation Skills

We have looked a bit at the basic areas for group observation and many more observation categories are presented in the pages that follow. The next question is how the observations should be recorded. Before I present the possibilities and we start looking at their strengths and weaknesses, let me make a plea to keep your observations simple and straightforward. In our training programs for group observers, I have them cut in half whatever they had planned to observe before they go into the field to do it as everyone wants to collect much more data than can ever be used. Keep it simple!!

In general, observations can be:

1. Put into predetermined categories (roles of group members)
2. Rated (survey of group development, behaviour frequency observation guide)
3. Tabulated in numerical frequencies (how many times each member spoke)
4. Charted (who spoke to whom, who sat next to whom, who paired with whom for a task)

5. Described in anecdotes (Howard arrived ten minutes late for the meeting and sat down giggling)
6. Recorded in a running account
7. Summarized in a narrative record (see outline later in this section)
8. Punched into a computer for later systematic analysis

As a participant observer or training observer, it is important that the observations and their recording doesn't get in the way of fairly full participation in the group. The observer can prepare for the task by looking the guide over before the session and becoming familiar with its categories or areas. When using it for the first few times, it is helpful to have the guide handy where it can be referred to during the meeting or perhaps for note-taking. After the group session, the observer will take some time to complete recording with the guide.

An observation record will be most useful if it separates objective descriptions from hunches and interpretations. In my observation records, for example, I put my subjective observations and hunches in parentheses (members seem to be getting tired of discussing this issue), and my interpretations in brackets [the group seems determined not to let Marilyn take over the group again today.] Usually I have a lot of questions to myself and the group, and this too I separate by putting in parentheses (Libby is sure talking a lot—what's got her going?) and (why has this budget issue come up again—wasn't it resolved in the last meeting?).

Observers may also be concerned about how they should present their material—guide sheet, recording pages—to the group and describe their role. Opinions vary about how this is best done, but my strong view is that a straightforward, materials on the table approach is most successful. Observers should briefly describe their interests in observing to the group and the areas they will be watching. When I am the observer, I also mention who will be reading my notes or how they will be used, and say that my notes can be read by members anytime. This serves as a convenient introduction to the group of the usefulness of process observations, and may stimulate members to do more thoughtful observing themselves. Members will then be more ready to hear the observers report, discuss it, and give their own observations about factors helping and hindering the work of the group.

When individuals approach me with questions between sessions, I express interest and suggest the person bring it up in the group so we can all hear the answers and talk about it. Or I'll get some reporting time in the group and then say that some people have been asking questions and talking about my last observer's report outside the group and ask what questions they'd want to discuss now that we are together. This helps to get the whole group into the process of discussions and gradually make it a more accepted use of group time.

If there is to be a training function for the group observer, the ideal situation is for the total group to work out the areas they want to have observed and either take turns being the observer or have a pair of observers do it for several sessions (to get some continuity and comparisons in their observations), and then to pass the task on to a new pair. In my consulting or program evaluation work with groups, I describe my observation and recording functions and then ask for a volunteer who will join me as an inside observer. This has always worked well in my experience, as the observer who is a regular participant in the group usually has insights that I, as a newcomer, don't have. In any case, the more interest and involvement that members have in the observation activity, the more likely that the information generated will be accepted by the group and used in its action planning.

It is important for the observers to find ways of conducting observations without disrupting the group activity or separating themselves from the group. Research on this concern indicates that observing and recording group behaviour and making records does not affect the group's operation if the observer is able to establish rapport with the group. Members and staff usually have this rapport and new members can build it by demonstrating real interest in the group's success; tuning in to the group and being open about how the observations will be used by the group and others.

My concerns are more about how much visibility and attention I, as an observer, want to have. If I am in a training observer function trying to motivate the whole group to spend more time and energy on process observation and feedback, I sit centre stage (it's hard to observe if you can't see everyone in the group) and record on 8-1/2 x 11 pages attached to a clip board or in a loose-leaf notebook. For situations where I want to minimize the attention paid to my observing/recording function, I either jot occasional notes on 3 x 5 cards or write in a 4 x 6-1/2 loose-leaf notebook I can slip in my back pocket.

The advent of inexpensive and compact camcorders has increased the use of video recordings as part of the group observation function. Certainly, the cost and size have changed the whole operation since I started using reel-to-reel video, huge cameras, and extra lighting twenty-five years ago, but most of the same weaknesses and strengths are still there. Cost is no longer a drawback, as it was to purchase the six to eight thousand dollars-worth of equipment with which I started (over twenty thousand of today's dollars). The major strength was seen as providing an unbiased record of the group's proceedings. This hasn't usually been the case, as a video camera can't take in the whole of most groups at the same time and the person controlling the camera must use her biases to decide what part of the action will be recorded (the assertive speaker, the out-of-field pair engaged in side talk, or the enthusiastic supporters in the front row).

The small size of the new camcorders and their ability to record in any amount of light has made them very unobtrusive. And the replay of the group's activity is accepted by all members as the camera doesn't lie. However, the time involved in getting the equipment operational, then finding segments of the meeting that are useful to replay (few groups can stand watching their whole meeting again), and finally discussing the meaning of the selected segments is rarely more productive for future action planning than a crisp, well focussed observer's report followed by a high involvement group discussion. Videos are probably the most useful when providing individuals with objective feedback about their behaviour, and helping the formal group observers check out the accuracy of their recordings. The use of video recordings in assessing personal growth and program evaluation is described in another book in this series, *A Simplified Guide to Program Evaluation.*[3]

One of the most useful contributions of video recording a group session is in helping the observer improve the quality and accuracy of her records. Watching the video while looking over the observation record of the group's meeting provides the observer with an unusual opportunity to check out perceptions with the very objective record on the tape. If the observer missed any significant incident during the meeting, this will show up in comparing the observation notes to the video recording. Another method of improving observations is to have a team of observers, two or three people, who can compare their notes and pick up on any missed areas. In several of my projects we asked our visitors to take on an observation role with the regular observer and share perceptions. This usually made the session more interesting for the visitor and gave the group the benefit of some fresh insights. Later I set up 'observation visitations' with teams of observers from parallel programs attending each other's sessions and reporting on their observations before they left.

The use of video recordings and co-observers are especially useful as training aides for people just learning observation methods, but they are also useful in checking and validating information collected through observations. It is always a good practice to try to get three different viewpoints or sources of information to confirm a major conclusion. This triangulation to check accuracy requires that a group observer look for two other sources of information such as the video recording, a co-observer, informal interviews with the participants, program records of the group, written questionnaires or surveys from the participants, or diaries or records kept by other group members. In practice it is usually best to have two independent observers who check their perceptions with the group and follow up by informally interviewing the members after the meeting. If the quality of the information is still in doubt, a three or four question Post Meeting Reaction questionnaire should complete the

---

3.   Hedley G. Dimock, *A Simplified Guide to Program Evaluation*, Rev. ed. (Guelph: University of Guelph Press, 1987). Distributed exclusively by Captus Press Inc., North York, Ont.

triangulation and establish beyond reasonable doubt the validity of the information. This kind of validation increases in importance if the information is to be used for comparisons between or among groups or for organization program evaluation purposes.

Another group observation concern is the balancing of observation areas such as content and process. Content refers to what the group is working on and what it is saying, while process looks at how the group is working. This is the analogy to the 'words and the music', where the words represent the overt task and concern of the group and the music reflects the real issues or concerns of the members (inclusion, control, intimacy) in working on these tasks. Over a period of time observers will want to get more 'music' into their observations by looking at what people say and do and trying to get at its real intent or meaning. Often the words of participants, if taken at face value, do not reveal their intended communication: "I think Judi has a good idea here but..." (real meaning, "I disagree"). "I'd like to get some clarification of Gervase's idea, did he mean..." (real meaning, "My opinion is..."). "Let me summarize the ideas presented to date" (one idea is given the spotlight which seems to be the idea with which the summarizer agrees). Or, if the group continues to flog a dead issue, the observer may feel it is flight behaviour to escape dealing with an intense, interpersonal conflict which has just surfaced. Member interactions should be taken as straightforwardly as possible, but if hunches or interpretations occur to the observer, they should be recorded, but clearly identified as hunches or interpretations (parentheses or brackets in my records).

In addition to balancing the observations of the content with the process, consideration should be given to balancing observations about individuals with those of the group as a whole. As excitement about an activity or issue increases, there is a tendency to watch the key players very carefully and sometimes miss what the lower intensity participants are doing, what they may be communicating through body language or non-verbal behaviour, or what the overall mood of the group is during the excitement. Checking over an observation guide periodically or setting up time sampling helps to balance observations. And there may even be a moment to note observations of what didn't happen.

Training Group Observers

As usual, experiential training or 'learning by doing' works best for training observers. Basic training can start with making observations and then discussing what was observed with others at the close of the session. More sophisticated training often has observers in training looking over several observation guides, trying out the ones that look interesting in order to gain practice with a broad variety of observation areas, and discussing observations with other observers in training after each practice session. The practice sessions are usually real groups that the trainees are working with, but they may start with simulated group meetings within the training group. Observers work most effectively and accurately if they design their own observation guide or major areas to observe and this activity should be facilitated within the training program. In my training programs, our last activity is for each person to work out an observation plan for observing and reporting on a real group that I bring in for everyone to observe, and then comparing results with the other observers and getting feedback from the demonstration group members.

A lot of group biases and value judgments are likely to appear during early practices. This is quite natural as most people quickly move their descriptive observations to a conclusion or evaluation so they can take action and it takes considerable practice to record the descriptions first. Observers will report "the room was too smokey" rather than noting that three people asked if the smoking could be limited and another person opened the window. Or, the observer may report that the setting was stimulating and appropriate rather than saying the group met in a library with the walls lined with books and the participants seated around a large rectangular table. In training sessions, observers pair up and exchange their observation reports. Each person identifies all the conclusions made by the other and asks for the descriptive data which led to making that conclusion. This practice is particularly valuable after an observer finds that in reporting to a real group, the descriptions are always safe and lead to further discussion, while the conclusions may arouse resentment and close the group off from the observer. While separating descriptions from value judgments sounds fairly easy, it takes most graduate students months to learn, and observer trainees require all of a two week residential program.

Observation Guide— Developmental Areas

Observation guides are something like road maps in that they can save a lot of time and energy and keep people moving into relatively unknown areas from 'driving in circles'. Even very experienced drivers will consult a road map to figure out the most desirable route to their destination. Some will take the shortest route and conserve on energy consumption, others will take the fastest route figuring that time is money, and some prefer the scenic route or try to avoid major congested areas with other reasons in mind. In any case, after travelling the areas many times the road map may be checked periodically to make sure something isn't being missed but it is usually put away. The following selection of guides and observation tools are very useful in exploring relatively new territory and checking from time to time that there aren't perhaps tougher but more productive pathways to group development available. In the long run they should be set aside as observers develop their

Group Observation Guide

Group _____ Date _____ Time ____to____ Observer _____

CLIMATE

(*Physical*) distractions   ventilation, lighting   seating arrangements conducive to interaction?

(*Emotional*)   formal—informal?   accepting—judgmental?
cooperative—competitive?   supportive?   friendly?   enthusiastic?
• Do members express feelings (fears, desires, concerns)?

INVOLVEMENT

• Why are members here?   absenteeism—lateness?
• Stake in present problem or activity?   Commitment to group?
• Attentive? (List who)   Restless?   Withdrawn?

INTERACTION

• Lines of communication (1 to 1, 1 to group, or all through leader)?
• Distribution of participation (what % of the group did half the talking)?   Overparticipators?   Underparticipators?
• Who has the power in the group?   Sub-groups or cliques?
• Impact of group size on interaction?
• Balance of task and group building roles?
                              % Task _____   % Group _____
• Are people listening and building on the ideas of others?
• Non-verbal Behaviour?   gestures—facial expression—posture?

COHESION

• Degree of group solidarity?   Group vs. individual interests?
• Group norms observed?   Who doesn't conform?   Strength of pressures to conform?   Readiness to accept majority decisions?
• How well does group work as a team?

PRODUCTIVITY

• Clarity of goals?   realistic—understood?   percent supporting goals?
• Did members contribute to statement of goals?
• Was there a flexible plan for reaching goal?   Understood by all?   Followed?
• Effectiveness of procedures and outcomes evaluated regularly?
• What steps did group use in making decisions?   Where did it get off track?
• Were decisions from last session carried out?   Started and stopped on time?
• Was next session planned for?   How?
• Effect of leader/chairperson, chief executive, recorder/secretary roles?
• Style of leadership?   Impact on participation?   Percent of content and process?
• Notes on productivity (content tags)

own guides based on the specific needs and problems of the groups with whom they are working.

Following the sequence of viewpoints of group development presented in the last section, the first guide is set up to remind the observer of the points to look for under the five major areas of a group's operation. This guide is designed for the sheet to be placed in front of the observer or stapled to a file folder and opened like a book, which makes it a bit easier to handle. Look at the guide on page 36 and you will notice a number of different sub-questions phrased in just a few words, leaving very little space for an extended answer. It is expected that the observer will glance over the guide sheet every little while during a meeting or activity and make a note or two of something that has become clear. Very little is written during the activity but the constant thinking about these areas plus the few notes enables the worker to complete the record or write it up in a narrative fashion after the meeting. After the observer is familiar with the categories, he can participate with the group in the normal way and not be tied down to making more than a few notes with the guide sheet. Watching and participating in the group comes first, making notes second.

Many of the questions raised in all five sections of this guide are appropriate ones to ask the group members or raise for discussion. "Were the problems we worked on today important ones to you?" "Why?" "Did you all understand our goal; what we were trying to accomplish?" "Did you feel any pressure to change your opinion and go along with the majority?" If this can be done it helps the worker check the observations.

Under the heading INTERACTION it is suggested that who speaks to whom is worth noting. Do the members usually talk to one or two people (the designated leader or the power figures); to a best friend, or to everyone? An additional page can be added for the interaction diagram and additional comments on roles of group members.

An interaction diagram also shows the diversity of participation and the amount for each person. Two five-minute samples during an hour's meeting usually provide a reasonably accurate picture of interaction, and can be corrected and generalized from after the meeting with the less precise observations made during the rest of the meeting. An easy form for showing interactions is illustrated in Figure 10 on the next page. The arrow shows the person to whom the remarks were directed, or, if they are addressed to the total group, the arrow stops in the middle. The number of times a person talked is tabulated by counting the number of arrows he sends out, plus the number of dash marks on each of the arrows. In Figure 10, King spoke twelve times and White did not participate. During this part of the meeting, the worker who was observing did not participate.

FIGURE 10 *An Interaction Diagram*

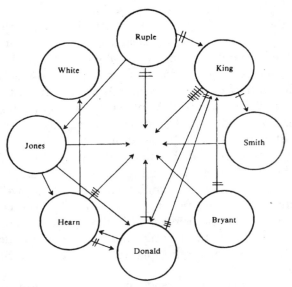

This diagram is of a small group based on two samples of 5 minutes each.

Appropriate group procedures are needed to facilitate decision making. The topics under the structure and effect of the chairman's role in the guide suggest observation of the factors often directly related to the inefficient and frustrating problem-solving procedures of a group.

Survey of Group Development

The tool called "Survey of Group Development" was designed for intermittent use with a group. The observer or staff person would ordinarily complete this form (seen on pages 41–43) after every few meetings and use it to chart the development of the group in these key areas. The tool has been used extensively by group participants as an aide to assessing and analyzing their group's operation. It is particularly useful for program evaluations and comparisons of programs in camps, social service, rehabilitation recreation, and informal educational programs. While the survey requires only thirteen ticks the average completion time is about twenty minutes.

Experience has shown that this survey is best completed following a group meeting or program activity, but the thirteen dimensions should be the focus for observations during the meeting. Some observers find it helpful to jot down the thirteen areas on a

Dimensions of Group Growth

The following is a comprehensive set of dimensions on which a group can be evaluated. The progress of the group in these thirteen areas provides a summary of its health.

1. **Unity** (Degree of unity, cohesion or "we-ness")
   - Is the group just a collection of individuals, or is there some common purpose and spirit based on friendships?

2. **Self-direction** (The group's own motive power)
   - Is the group apathetic, dominated by a single person, or self-propelled with all the members initiating?

3. **Group climate** (The extent to which members feel free to be themselves)
   - Are people inhibited and "up tight", or do they feel free to express their needs and desires within the framework of the total group's welfare?

4. **Distribution of leadership** (Extent to which leadership roles are distributed among members)
   - Does one or a few members take leadership, or is leadership shared by all the members?

5. **Distribution of responsibility** (Extent to which responsibility is shared among members)
   - Do members tend to shirk responsibility with one or two always carrying things out, or is responsibility distributed among all the members?

6. **Problem solving** (Group's ability to think straight, make use of everyone's ideas and decide creatively about its problems)
   - Is decision making hasty or erratic with confused movement towards decisions, or is there a good pooling of ideas with an orderly pattern for decision making?

7. **Method of resolving disagreements with group** (How group works out disagreements)
   - Does one person arbitrarily resolve differences, is there a majority vote with the strongest sub-group dominating, or are there compromises and attempts to work out a consensus?

8. **Meets basic needs** (Extent to which group gives a sense of security, achievement, approval, recognition and belonging)
   - Does the group experience add a little or a great deal to meeting the basic needs of all members?

9. **Variety of activities**
   - Are there dull routines with little variety of activity, or are different approaches tried that lead to considerable variety?

10. **Depth of activities** (Extent to which activities are gone into in such a way that members can use full potentials, skills and creativity)
    - Are the activities or discussions conducted in a superficial way, or is there real depth with members being challenged to develop their abilities?

11. **Leader-member rapport** (Relations between the group and the designated leader)
    - Is the group indifferent toward the leader, is there "hero-worship" of him, or is he integrated and accepted as a person in his own right?

12. **Role of the leader** (Extent to which the group is centred about the designated leader)
    - Does the group revolve around the interests and personality of the leader, or do the members "carry the ball" themselves?

13. **Stability**
    - Is there a high absenteeism and turnover, or is the group stable in terms of the conditions under which it operates?

three by five card and glance over them during the meeting as a reminder.

As observers become more familiar with the thirteen dimensions and skilled in their observations related to them, they find the four choices for each area do not allow them to record their real assessments. At this point they should either modify the suggested descriptions by changing a word here and there, or write up their own summary under each of the headings (see Dimensions of Group Growth starting on the previous page).

However, if the survey is to be used for measurement and comparison purposes, modifications of the descriptions are not appropriate and observers should go back to selecting the box which most nearly describes the group. Comparisons of these critical areas of a group's development over a period of time provides a rather accurate measurement of a group's growth, as well as an indicator of group health and usefulness for program evaluation. It may seem that this survey is subject to observer judgment or bias, yet our research has shown that independent observers have a high inter-observer reliability (significant at .05 level) and that ratings by members, leaders, and supervisors correlate at the same high level of significance.

Survey of Group Development

Group _____ Date _____ Observer _____

For each area, place an "X" in the box which most nearly describes the group.

1. UNITY (Degree of unity, cohesion or "we-ness")

☐ Group is just a collection of individuals or sub-groups; little group feeling.

☐ Group is very close and there is little room or felt need for other contacts and experience.

☐ Some group feeling. Unity stems more from external factors than from real friendship.

☐ Strong common purpose and spirit based on real friendships. Group usually sticks together.

2. SELF-DIRECTION (The group's own motive power)

☐ Little drive from anywhere, either from members or designated leader.

☐ Domination from a strong single member, a clique, or the designated leader.

☐ Group has some self-propulsion but needs considerable push from designated leader.

☐ Initiation, planning, executing, and evaluating comes from total group.

3. GROUP CLIMATE (The extent to which members feel free to be themselves)

☐ Climate inhibits good fun, behaviour and expression of desire, fears and opinions.

☐ Members freely express needs and desires; joke, tease and argue to detriment of the group.

☐ Members express themselves but without observing interests of total group.

☐ Members feel free to express themselves but limit expression to total group welfare.

4. DISTRIBUTION OF LEADERSHIP (Extent to which leadership roles are distributed among members)

☐ A few members always take leadership roles. The rest are passive.

☐ Many members take leadership but one or two are continually followers.

☐ Some of the members take leadership roles but many remain passive followers.

☐ Leadership is shared by all members of the group.

5. DISTRIBUTION OF RESPONSIBILITY (Extent to which responsibility is shared among members)

☐ Everyone tries to get out of jobs.

☐ Many members accept responsibilities but do not carry them out.

☐ Responsibility carried by a few members.

☐ Responsibilities are distributed among and carried out by nearly all members.

41

6. PROBLEM SOLVING (Group's ability to think straight, make use of everyone's ideas and decide creatively about its problems)

☐ Not much thinking as a group. Decisions made hastily, or group lets leader or worker do most of the thinking.

☐ Some thinking as a group but not yet an orderly process.

☐ Some cooperative thinking but group gets tangled up in pet ideas of a few. Confused movement toward solutions.

☐ Good pooling of ideas and orderly thought. Everyone's ideas are used to reach final plan.

7. METHOD OF RESOLVING DISAGREEMENTS WITH GROUP (How group works out disagreements)

☐ Group waits for the designated leader to resolve disagreements.

☐ Compromises are effected by each sub-group giving up something.

☐ Strongest sub-group dominates through a vote and majority rule.

☐ Group as a whole arrives at a solution that satisfies all members and which is better than any single suggestion.

8. MEETS BASIC NEEDS (Extent to which group gives a sense of security, achievement, approval, recognition and belonging)

☐ Group experience adds little to the meeting of most members' needs.

☐ Group experience contributes substantially to basic needs of most members.

☐ Group experience contributes to some degree to basic needs of most members.

☐ Group contributes substantially to basic needs of all members.

9. VARIETY OF ACTIVITIES

☐ Little variety in activities—stick to same things.

☐ Considerable variety in activities. Try out new activities.

☐ Some variety in activities.

☐ Great variety in activities. Continually trying out new ones.

10. DEPTH OF ACTIVITIES (Extent to which activities are gone into in such a way that members can use full potentials, skills and creativity)

☐ Little depth in activities—just scratching the surface.

☐ Considerable depth in activities. Members able to utilize some of their abilities.

☐ Some depth but members are not increasing their skills.

☐ Great depth in activities. Members find each a challenge to develop their abilities.

11. LEADER-MEMBER RAPPORT (Relations between the group and the designated leader)

☐ Antagonistic or resentful.

☐ Friendly and interested. Attentive to leader's suggestions.

☐ Indifferent towards leader. Friendship neither sought nor rejected. Non-communicative.

☐ Intimate relations: openness and sharing. Strong rapport.

12. ROLE OF THE LEADER (Extent to which the group is centred about the designated leader)

☐ Activities, discussion, and decisions revolve about interests, desires and needs of leader.

☐ Leader acts as stimulator—suggests ideas or other ways of doing things. Helps group find ways of making own decisions.

☐ Group looks to leader for suggestions and ideas. Leader decides, when member gets in a jam.

☐ Leader stays out of discussion and makes few suggestions of things to do. Lets members carry the ball themselves.

13. STABILITY

☐ High absenteeism and turnover; influences group a great deal.

☐ Some absenteeism and turnover with minor influence on group.

☐ High absenteeism and turnover; little influence on group growth.

☐ Low absenteeism rate and turnover. Group very stable.

Roles of Group Members

This is one of the most popular observation tools as it encourages descriptions of individual behaviour and makes for specific feedback to each member. Leadership training groups find practicing different roles and getting feedback on the practice very useful in developing a larger repertoire of roles, and in gaining skill and comfort in when to use them. Groups trying to increase their effectiveness will have the observer focus on the total group (not identifying individual roles), and perhaps show a frequency chart to illustrate the overplayed roles and the ones rarely taken that the group might want to work at adding.

To make a complete record of a meeting using this guide (seen on pages 44–45) is a full-time job and removes the observer from participating. To be a participant-observer, time samples can be used for intensive recording. A five minute sample every fifteen or twenty minutes works out pretty well. It is best if the time samples are determined ahead of time to increase the likelihood of their being a cross-section of the total meeting. Observing with roles of group members compliments video recording of a group as both forms of observation make for specific feedback to individuals. This activity is particularly useful for training purposes where the goal is personal learning and skill development for individual members such as group dynamics classes, leadership and management training, and personal growth groups.

Let us now look at a couple of technical problems that come up in using this observation guide. More than one role is often taken as participant speaks and it is difficult to decide how to categorize the input. A person may start off seeming to agree and build on a previous speaker's idea but ends up making a new proposal. Is this

Roles of Group Members—
Definition Sheet

TASK FUNCTIONS

1. **Defines problems**—group problem is defined: overall purpose of group is outlined.

2. **Seeks information**—requests factual information about group problem or methods of procedure, or for clarification of suggestions.

3. **Gives information**—offers facts or general information about group problem, methods to be used, or clarifies a suggestion.

4. **Seeks opinions**—asks for the opinions of others relevant to discussion.

5. **Gives opinions**—states beliefs or opinions relevant to discussion.

6. **Tests feasibility**—questions reality, checks practicality of suggested solutions.

GROUP BUILDING AND MAINTENANCE FUNCTIONS

7. **Coordinating**—a recent statement is clarified and related to another statement in such a way as to bring them together. Proposed alternatives are reviewed for the group.

8. **Mediating-harmonizing**—interceding in disputes or disagreements and attempting to reconcile them. Highlights similarities in views.

9. **Orienting-facilitating**—keeps group on the track, points out deviations from agreed upon procedures or from direction of group discussion. Helping group process along, proposing other structures or procedures to make group more effective.

10. **Supporting-encouraging**—expressing approval of another's suggestion, praising others' ideas, being warm and responsive to ideas of others.

11. **Following**—going along with the movement of the group, accepting ideas of others, expressing agreement.

INDIVIDUAL FUNCTIONS

12. **Blocking**—interfering with the progress of the group by arguing, resisting and disagreeing beyond reason. Or, by coming back to same "dead" issue later. Taking up air time.

13. **Out of field**—withdrawing from discussion, daydreaming, doing something else, whispering to others, leaving room, etc.

14. **Digressing**—getting off the subject, leading discussion in some "personally oriented direction", or expanding a brief statement into a long nebulous speech.

Roles of Group Members

Put initials of each member at top of each column.

TASK ROLES										
• Defines problem										
• Seeks information										
• Gives information										
• Seeks opinions										
• Gives opinions										
• Tests feasibility										
GROUP BUILDING & MAINTENANCE ROLES										
• Coordinating										
• Mediating-Harmonizing										
• Orienting-Facilitating										
• Supporting-Encouraging										
• Following										
INDIVIDUAL ROLES										
• Blocking										
• Out of Field										
• Digressing										

If a general, rather than individual picture of the group is desired, the first column can be used to show the total times that function was taken by any group member. This would then show what functions were being over-played and under-played in the group.

to be categorized as supporting-encouraging or gives opinions? While it is possible to list this contribution under both categories, my rule of thumb is to list it under the chief message it left with the group. In this case it would be 'gives opinions' as a new proposal has more impact than some general agreement. Thus, "I am in general agreement with Noela's proposal which I think this group has the resources to implement, yet I wonder if we might not do better having our own presentation and display two or three weeks later" (gives opinions). Or a question may be followed with a new proposal. "Why do some members want to have us attend city council and propose that they assist us with some special funding? Wouldn't we be better off with a major story in the newspaper or on local television?" (gives opinions). If in doubt, the observer could list them under both categories and in the long run the group profile of roles would look pretty much the same.

It is more difficult to categorize an intervention when the true meaning is given a verbal camouflage, especially if it is a fairly long speech. While the content of the intervention should be taken at face value and categorized accordingly, my rule of thumb is that, when in doubt, either list it as giving opinions or just omit it form the record. Often, the tendency for a new observer is to puzzle over the intervention for a bit, and by then the next speaker may say something that influences the rating. For example, if Tom rambles on and it is not clear whether he is supporting a previous idea, giving information about it, or seeking others' opinions about it, and the next speaker says, "Yes, I too agree that this would make sense and that we should do it", there may be an influence to categorize Tom as giving opinions (agreement) or supporting-encouraging. The rule of thumb here is to try not to be influenced by a following statement in categorizing the previous one.

All of the task- and group-building roles can be helping or hindering the group—appropriateness to the situation and timing are the keys. Giving opinions, for example, before the problem is clear to everyone, may not be helpful yet if it clarifies the problem for some members, it may. But testing feasibility before the problem is clear to everyone would not be helpful. Generally, the individual roles are not likely to be helpful and in the early days of working with this guide, I called them non-functional roles. However, I found this was not always the case as an "out of field" joke often broke the tension, and a "digression" might end up having some value at a later point of time. And a "digression" for the observer might be an important contribution for several members.

The Behaviour Frequency Observation Guide, like the Roles of Group Members Guide, is most useful in groups where indicators of the growth of individual members are needed, or in training, treatment and personal development groups where feedback on individual behaviour is appropriate. Consequently, this format has been used extensively in alternative educational programs for youth,

Behaviour Frequency Observation Guide

Group _____ Date _____ Observer _____

Rate the frequency of each person's behaviour using:
0 = not observed
1 = once or twice
2 = a few times
3 = frequently

NAMES						
1. Initiated activities						
2. Assumed leadership in group						
3. Made friendly approaches to others						
4. Withdrawn or out of group						
5. Got angry and shouted or sulked						
6. Showed vim and enthusiasm for activity						
7. Showed off, boasted, seeked attention						
8. Disrupted or disturbed group						
9. Fidgets, twitches, appears nervous						
10. Helped others to participate or learn						
11. Helped group to evaluate its performance						
12. Praised or supported others						

camp groups, classrooms, growth groups and in leadership and management training. Typically two or three members volunteer to complete the observation guide, or it may be used by the staff person and outside observer in a program evaluation project. The specific observational areas described in the guide may be revised to focus on the actual goals and objectives of the groups under study. This guide is most useful when it is completed by more than one observer over a fair length of time in which several ratings have been made.

A shorter version of the Narrative Record idea, is the Survey of Group Activity form (shown on page 49) which is particularly useful for groups that meet once a week or for groups undergoing some constant evaluation process such as treatment or therapy. It is also useful as a supervisory tool when the designated leader is in training and the group experience is part of that training (group leader trainee, student teacher or nurse, graduate student or camp counselor).

Types of Descriptions a Narrative Record Should Contain

1. A description of the setting, who was present and what the group did.
   a) A description of activities (*what* the group did).
   b) A description of feelings and emotions around the activities (*how* they did it).
   c) A description of how the activities came into being (member planning session, spontaneous, agency planned, etc.).

2. A description of the group's planning process. (This should tell not just what was discussed, but how the group planned and how decisions were reached).

3. A description of how the members functioned as a group.
   a) Degree of cohesiveness (unity vs. cliques, conflicts and individual behaviour).
   b) Distribution of task-responsibility roles (few, some or all) and how these roles were decided on (take turns, volunteer, appoint, etc.).

4. A description of individual members in the group.
   a) Group adjustment.
      1. Analysis of acceptance by group.
      2. Typical roles in group interaction (leadership, responsibility, non-functional behaviour, individual roles).
      3. Typical roles in group planning.
   b) Participant learning or skill development (these may be technical skills—learn to make copper ashtray) or human relations skills (learn to accept wise remarks from others).
   c) Individual behaviour.

5. Role of designated leader in group life. Description of:
   a) Areas of direction and control.
   b) Areas of limit setting and endorsing.
   c) Areas of stimulating and suggesting.
   d) Areas of showing technical knowhow (how to write an accident report or play a game).
   e) Areas of facilitating (helping things to come about).
   f) Use of relationships to influence individual behaviour (modelling).

6. Relation of group to other groups, the organization, or the community.

Other Observation Areas

A number of other observation areas are listed at this time which the interested worker may want to use in cafeteria style, picking out additional categories to look at or in starting from scratch to build his

Survey of Group Activity

Group _____ Date _____ Observer _____

1. Briefly describe what the group did:

2. General reaction of the group and individuals to these activities:

3. How did the group plan? How were decisions made or activities decided on?

4. Description of group relationships (subgrouping or pairing, dependency, conflict, power plays, use of group pressure, group building):

5. Description of individual's behaviour (cooperative, out of field, seeking attention—anything unusual or a problem):

own observation guide. The items are in no particular order and are in addition to the areas mentioned in the previous guide sheets though there is some overlapping.

Always included in any collection of observation areas are:

- Power/Control; and
- Recognition/Status.

These are the two most powerful motivators in groups.

1. *Group rules* (standards)—procedures for handing routines, dealing with absences, lateness, poor completion of jobs assigned, etc.

2. Clarity of members in expressing ideas.

3. How does the designated leader handle group problems?

4. Does the designated leader show favouritism among members?

5. List the members according to their status in the group.

6. How sensitive is the designated leader to the needs and interests of the members?

7. Method of control used by group.

8. Methods of resolving differences used by group.

9. Non-verbal communication—gestures (nodding head, tapping fingers), facial expressions (bored, surprised, disgusted), posture and position in relation to group.

10. Seating arrangement—who sits next to whom, who sits or participates on the fringe of the group, who is always centrally located, who often leaves group.

11. Who talks after whom (a great way to spot pairing and competition).

12. Critical incidents during activity.

13. Tension release through exuberant laughter or horseplay.

14. List position of members on controversial topic and identify subgroups and pairing.

15. How well was the program planned?

16. Use of available resources outside group (agency, community).

17. Leadership style of designated leader (directing, coaching, facilitating, delegating).

18. Respect and regard for facilities and equipment.

19. Hidden agenda.

20. Invisible committees.

21. Pressures for and against making a decision.

22. Stressing of pride in the group.

23. Setting clear and attainable goals.

24. Arranging goals and work methods so that the group succeeds.

25. Helping each member to be aware of his/her contribution to group success.

26. Sex roles and stereotypes (male, female, androgynous).

Group Records

Group workers, teachers and team leaders keep records of the growth of their groups in order to help the group grow and use the full potential of its members. As the workers make their observations of their groups and jots them down aided by the observation guides presented in this book, they start to develop a longitudinal picture of the growth of the groups and their present status. This picture may be supplemented with additional data from the other methods described in *How to Analyze and Evaluate Group Growth*[4]. These group records form the basis for the analysis of the group's strengths and weaknesses and the designated leaders' attempts to optimize their coaching roles. These records form the basis for any kind of systematic or planned group development. They may also be used to measure the results of the group experience for its members, provide information for annual reports and interpretive statements of the agency, and to help to orient a new worker to the group in the future. Group records provide a basis for supervision that is focused on helping the worker understand the group and improve its effectiveness in achieving the organization's goals. The major records for the worker to keep include: Survey of Group Development (the major dimensions of group growth), Behaviour Frequency Observation Guide (major value dimensions of individual growth), and Survey of Member Activity. These three are supplemented by the more extensive group observation records described here; and the sociometric measures, member and parent ratings, interest finders, member reactions, and other personal data described in *How to Analyze and Evaluate Group Growth*.

Two other forms of records have not been mentioned: anecdotal records and narrative descriptions. These methods have traditionally been popular with nurses, teachers and therapists. Essentially, an anecdotal record describes, in purely objective terms, an interesting or unusual event that happened either to an individual, a sub-group, or to the total group. Areas to consider for the possible writing of anecdotes have been described under observation headings; the major difference is the method of recording. The job of the recorder is to select incidents worth reporting and describe them objectively. These incidents should describe a wide range of behaviour, both

---

4. Hedley G. Dimock, *How to Analyze and Evaluate Group Growth*, 2nd ed. (Guelph: University of Guelph Press, 1985). Distributed exclusively by Captus Press Inc., North York, Ont.

positive and negative, of individuals in the group and of total group dynamics. Single incidents do not have much meaning but as the anecdotes accumulate, they have real value as they present an over-a-period-of-time, objective set of descriptions which can be used for diagnostic and comparative purposes. One of the best things about anecdotal records is that as they are brief descriptions of something that happened, people who were not part of the group can read them and make independent judgments about what was going on. These outside 'judges' may be classmates, other agency staff, or supervisors, and their role is to help the observer check out possible bias by giving an independent summary or analysis of what they think is going on in the group. This approach is part of the triangulation method of increasing the accuracy of observation information by trying to get three different views of an event or group characteristic. Procedures for using judges' ratings of anecdotal records for measurement and program evaluation are described in the *Simplified Guide to Program Evaluation* book in this series.

Anecdotes should be dated to establish their sequence in time, and the setting or activity of the group should be mentioned to put the description in context. Identifying the noise, lack of concentration, and silly antics of a group comes into perspective only if it is recorded that it was the evening of the last day of school for the year. Each anecdote should be reported in a factual, objective way. Value judgment or interpretations by the recorder are best omitted unless they are necessary to make the picture clear.

Examples of Useful Anecdotes

- In the club meeting today the boys' group discussed plans for their Christmas party and which girls they would invite. Pierre did not participate in the discussion. He fidgeted in his chair and wiggled his fingers. He was the first to leave at the close of the meeting.

- As the group came back from the ballfield after losing the game the boys became more and more quiet. Finally, after a period of silence, Hank said "we should have won the damn game anyway". Tears streaked down his cheek. George and Tim wept a little too.

- The eleven members of the board sat around a large table in low chairs and each member had a thick folder of papers in front of her. After opening the meeting, Libby (Chair) asked members to get out the consultants' report on revitalizing the association. It took three or four minutes for everyone to find the document in their large collections of papers. Libby made several attempts to start the discussion but couldn't get going until all had found the document.

Narrative or descriptive records are kept in diary form with the worker describing what happened and how she felt and reacted to these happenings. These records are usually written shortly after the time span to be reported on (a meeting or a day in a residential setting) has elapsed. The guide on page 48 "Types of Descriptions a Narrative Record Should Contain" will be helpful here. Added to this is the basic information about the group, names of those present, time and place of meeting, setting of meeting, and other conditions affecting the meeting (weather, holiday, exam period, etc.). The focus of the narrative record is on the group process—how members reacted to one another and to the designated leader—and not as much on the program content. The major weakness of narrative records is the time involved in writing them up, but this can be considerably reduced by tape recording the narrative description (small cassette recorders are best), and having a typist type up the records later. The other problem with narrative and anecdotal records is the difficulty most people have writing non-judgmental descriptions. Learning to do it represents a considerable investment of time (graduate students rarely learn it in a thirteen week course) and it is likely only worthwhile for those planning to use the methods extensively.

Records are an accepted part of systematic group work and of educational supervision, but the question raised by many students and beginning workers is "what records should I keep?" The most honest answer is "those records that will help you to work with the group more effectively in order that it can achieve its objectives and the agency's goals". There is no general answer as the background and training of the worker and the unique aspects of the group make a great deal of difference. Volunteer workers with little professional background will want simple, straightforward records that will gradually increase their understanding. Advanced professional workers doing intensive work, and trying to improve their practice or doing research will want complete records combining most of the material described in these two sections. Be encouraged to make your own choices.

My own opinion has been to encourage workers in the many different organizations where I have worked or been a consultant to use three surveys (Survey of Group Development, either of the individual surveys—Roles of Group Members or Behaviour Frequency Observation Guide, and Survey of Member Activity) as the basic records and to supplement these with other information, especially friendship finders or social relations indexes, as the situation appears to warrant it. In settings where there is a major emphasis on educational supervision, the narrative record is very useful for the worker's growth, as it allows the worker to describe things in his own words, and is more flexible than check off sheets. Our rule continues to be to not collect more data than we can use, but to try to expand our resources and develop our skills wherever possible.

Reporting Observations to Your Group

There is a great challenge in reporting observations to your group in your role as a *process-observer* or training observer that has more to do with the way you present your material than with the quality of your material. Groups like to feel that their observer, or anyone help-ing to process group experiences, is working on an assignment by the group and is responsible to the group for that task. It is a service role much like the group recorder who makes a report on the content of the group's meetings and looks for additions and corrections. The excitement of the observer role and the opportunity to watch individual roles and overall group operation makes it easy to move to a judg-mental or evaluative stance in reporting group observations. This tends to distance the observer from the group by setting her up as an evaluator who tells the group, and individuals, what has been going wrong. The group may react by rejecting the observers report actively— that is, arguing against it. Or they may reject it passively by politely thanking the observer and than quickly going on to the next item of business. After two or three such experiences the group finds it 'doesn't have time' for the observer's report, and looking at the group's process becomes a low priority and gradually disappears as a group activity.

that have continuing success with an observer function usually share it around the group with each member taking turns to report on from one to four group meetings. In an effect to move the observer's report from a lecture on what the group did that was helpful and not helpful, many groups either assign two observers or expect everyone to be a *participant-observer* and turn the observer report into a group discussion with many participants sharing their perception of what happened at the meeting and how it felt for them. As I mentioned earlier, when I am the *training-observer* or the *program-observer* (research-observer) I enlist a group member to join me in the observer role as this helps to get a member perspective on group process. It also encourages other members to participate in the discussion of the observers' report.

As an observer, it is helpful to make a few provocative observa-tions of key areas of the group's process in a descriptive rather than interpretive or judgmental fashion. Think of yourself as announcing a hockey game on radio, sports announcer style; describing as accurately as possible the key plays in the game with enough animation to keep all your listeners on the edge of their seats. Too much data, even if it is accurate and of high quality, is boring and counter-productive. Your goal is to present a crisp yet comprehensive report that is tan-talizing and will provoke members to respond in a general discussion. Figure 11 suggests how this might be done.

This provocative stage is furthered if you present your observa-tions in a descriptive way and then raise a number of questions about them. If you are prone to make interpretations, try to make

FIGURE 11 *Observer Report Example*

CONTENT OBSERVATION (factual report)	PROGRESS OBSERVATION (non-judgmental description)	PROCESS COMMENT (observer's hunches)	RESULTS OF OBSERVATIONS AND PROCESS COMMENT
The group made a number of suggestions for revisions to the vacation plan. None of them gained very much accepted.	All of the suggested revisions came from senior staff. Junior staff did not participate in discussion (many appeared bored)	"It seems all the suggestions and discussion came from senior staff. I wonder why none of the newer staff contributed to the discussion?"	Most of the newer people felt it was not their place to discuss vacation schedules. They felt that to do so would appear presumptuous to senior staff. When these feelings were made clear the discussion proceeded with input from the junior staff.
The proposed plan and schedule for dealing with next year's budget was discussed for fifty minutes. No decision was made about it.	Four times the group went through the same cycle of reviewing the proposal's strengths and weaknesses with no new data emerging.	"I'm wondering if the group finds the proposal unacceptable or is just trying to avoid the whole budget issue or really wants to deal with the proposal for the experimental program first?"	The group agreed that they were avoiding the budget issue because of the difficulty of the needed cutbacks. They agreed to first clear the deck of the experimental program proposal and then really buckle down and start with the budget issues.

two or three possible interpretations of the same event so that others can join in trying to figure out what was happening, and why. Or try to pose your interpretations as hunches or questions—"Estelle was very emotional in her participation today, and I wonder if that was related to what was going on in the group, or to something outside the group." "Irene made a number of interventions today that tried to keep us on track and accomplishing our tasks of recruiting new members. I'm not sure if this was an important task for her, or if she just wanted to complete it as quickly as possible." "Dick, Bob, and Sylvia raised a number of issues today about the use of our Planned Programming Budget System, but I wasn't sure if they were meant to help us use the process more effectively or if they were designed to question our continued use of the PPBS approach." "The group seemed to be very lighthearted tonight and I don't know if it was related to the difficulty of the task, or just a reflection that this is our first board meeting in a while when we haven't had a very heavy agenda." The role of the observer is to provide data that the group can use to increase its effectiveness, and the more the group can identify with the data and get excited by it, the more likely it is to be used in group planning.

Bibliography

Bennis, Warren G. "Patterns and vicissitudes in T-group development" in *T.-Group Theory and Laboratory Method* ed. L. Bradford et al., 248–278. New York: Wiley, 1964.

Bion, W.R. *Experiences in Groups*. New York: Basic Books, 1961.

Dimock, Hedley G. *Groups: Leadership and Group Development*. San Diego, CA: University Associates, 1987.

———, *How to Analyze and Evaluate Group Growth*, 2nd Edition. Guelph: University of Guelph Press, 1985.

Gibb, Jack R. *Trust: A New Theory of Personal and Organizational Development*. Los Angeles: Guild of Tudors Press, 1978.

Hare, A. Paul. *Handbook of Small Group Research*, 2nd Edition. New York: Free Press, 1976.

Heyens, R. and Lippitt, R. "Systematic observational techniques" in *Handbook of Social Psychology* ed. G. Lindzey, 370–404. Reading, Mass.: Addison-Wesley, 1954.

Heyens, R. and Zander, A. "Observation of Group Behaviour" in *Research Methods in the Behavioral Sciences* eds. L. Festinger and D. Katz, 381–417. New York: Dryden, 1953.

Kormanski, Charles L. "A Situational Leadership® approach to groups using the Tuckman model of group development" in *The 1985 Annual: Developing Human Resources* eds. L.D. Goodstein and J.W. Pfeiffer. San Diego, CA: University Associates, 1985.

Miles, Matthew B. *Learning to Work in Group*, 2nd Edition. New York: Teachers College, 1981.

Napier, Rodney and Gershenfeld, Matti. *Groups: Theory and Experience*, 2nd Edition. Boston: Houghton-Mifflin, 1981.

Pattern, Michael Q. *Qualitative Evaluation Methods*. Beverly Hills, CA: Sage, 1980.

Preiffer, J. William. *Theories and Models in Applied Behavioral Science*, Volume II—Groups. San Diego, CA: Pfeiffer & Co., 1991.

Schutz, William C. *FIRO—A Three Dimensional Theory of Interpersonal Behaviour*. Reprinted as *The Interpersonal Underworld*. Palo Alto, CA: Science and Behaviour Books, 1966; and Mill Valley, CA: Will Schutz Associates, 1989.

Shaw, Marvin E. *Group Dynamics*, 3rd Edition. New York: McGraw-Hill, 1981.

Tuckman, B.W. and Jensen, M.A.C. "Stages of small group development revisited", *Group and Organizational Studies* 2, no. 4 (1977): 419–427.

Zander, Alvin. *Making Groups Effective*. San Francisco: Jossey-Bass, 1982.

———, "Systematic Observation of small face-to-face groups" in *Research Methods in Social Relations* M. Jahada et al., 516–538. New York: Dryden, 1951.